THE ELEMENTS

Silver

Susan Watt

BENCHMARK BOOKS

MARSHALL CAVENDISH
NEW YORK

Benchmark Books
Marshall Cavendish
99 White Plains Road
Tarrytown, New York 10591

www.marshallcavendish.com

Library of Congress Cataloging-in-Publication Data

Watt, Susan, date.
Silver / by Susan Watt.
p.   cm. — (The elements)
Includes index.
Summary: Explores the history of silver and explains its chemistry, its uses, and its
importance in our lives.
ISBN 0-7614-1464-9
1. Silver—Juvenile literature. [1. Silver.] I. Title. II. Elements
(Benchmark Books)
QD181.A3 W37 2003
546'.654—dc21
2002006080

Printed in Hong Kong.

Picture credits
Front cover: Killer Stock Inc. at Corbis
Back cover: José Manuel Sanchis at Corbis
AKG: Pieter Bruegel 4; Hans Hesse 8
Corbis: Hulton Archive 10; Lester V. Bergman 14 (*left*), 14 (*right*), 30; Killer Stock Inc. 17;
Kevin R. Morris 20; Charles O'Rear 16; Charles E. Rotkin *iii*, 7;
José Manuel Sanchis 9 (*bottom*); Adam Woolfitt 11
Sylvia Cordaiy: Dizzy De Silva 22
Hulton Archive: 19, 21
Imaging Body: 12
NASA: 25
PhotoDisc (45): 27
Science Photo Library: Jim Amos 13; Andrew Syred *i*, 6; Pascal Goetgheluck 9 (*top*)
Stone: Phil Degginger 24
USDA: 26
Werner Forman Archive: The Egyptian Museum, Cairo 18

Series created by Brown Partworks Ltd.
Designed by Sarah Williams

Contents

What is silver?

Silver has been prized since the days of the earliest civilizations. Next to gold, silver was considered the most valuable of all the metals. The delicate, almost creamy whiteness and rarity of the metal made it the natural choice to represent wealth in the form of small, transportable tokens we now call coins. Since medieval times, laws in many countries have protected the status of this precious metal. All goods made of silver still need to be tested and stamped before they can be sold.

We all have something made of silver. Silver is all around us—even if we cannot always see it is there. Batteries, computer keyboards, light switches, photographic paper, solar cells, and water purifiers all contain silver or its compounds. While there is little doubt that the metal will always be valued for its bright, shiny appearance, the continued use of silver as a practical material also seems assured.

Early chemists—called alchemists—likened silver to the Moon due to the metal's lustrous appearance. Before the modern chemical symbols were invented, silver was represented by a moon-shaped crescent.

The silver atom

Every element is made up of tiny particles called atoms. Atoms contain even smaller particles called protons, neutrons, and electrons. The protons and neutrons cluster together in the dense nucleus at the center of an atom. The electrons revolve around the nucleus in a series of layers called electron shells.

The number of protons is given by the atomic number. Silver's atomic number is 47, so there are 47 positively charged protons in each atom. The number of electrons and protons is always the same, which means there are 47 negatively

DID YOU KNOW?

ISOTOPES

Every silver atom is made up of 47 protons and 47 electrons, but there may be different numbers of neutrons in its nucleus. Atoms of an element with the same number of protons and electrons, but different numbers of neutrons, are called isotopes. Two different isotopes of silver occur in nature. Around 52 percent of all silver atoms have 60 neutrons in their nuclei. The remaining 48 percent contain 62 neutrons in the nucleus. Other silver isotopes do occur. Some contain as few as 56 neutrons, while others have up to 66 neutrons. These isotopes are unstable, radioactive atoms that break down quickly into other atoms. They do not occur naturally.

SILVER ATOM

Nucleus

First shell
Second shell
Third shell
Fourth shell
Fifth shell

Every silver atom has 47 electrons, which revolve around the nucleus in 5 electron shells. There are 2 electrons in the first (inner) shell, 8 electrons in the second shell, 18 electrons in the third and fourth shells, and 1 in the outer, or valence, shell.

charged electrons revolving around the nucleus of each silver atom. Neutrons are about the same size as protons but have no electrical charge. Different silver atoms may contain different numbers of neutrons in the nucleus.

Special characteristics

Silver has many unusual characteristics. For example, pure silver conducts both heat and electricity better than any other substance. It also reflects visible light very well, which has led to its use in mirrors and in applications where protection from the Sun's rays is needed. In other ways silver is much less unusual. Silver's density is average for a metal, unlike the high density of the precious metals gold and platinum. These metals are almost twice as dense as silver. This is why a silver ring feels lighter than a gold ring of the same size. The melting point of silver is also low.

SILVER FACTS	
Name	Silver
Chemical symbol	Ag
Type of element	Metal
Color	Silver
Atomic number	47
Atomic mass	107.87
Melting point	1,763° F (962° C)
Boiling point	3,923° F (2,162° C)

A scanning electron micrograph shows crystals of pure silver (magnified x 850).

In terms of its chemistry, silver is rather unreactive. But this is one of silver's useful features. Unlike iron, silver does not react with oxygen in the air. This makes it useful as a corrosion-free material. It also makes it safe to touch. We can even eat from it in the form of tableware and cutlery. Silver also forms many compounds that have useful properties, such as silver halides (silver combined with a halogen—an element such as bromine, chlorine, or iodine) used in photography.

One unusual characteristic of silver is that it is remarkably permeable to oxygen. Silver atoms soak up oxygen molecules in the air like a sponge soaks up water, particularly when the silver atoms are hot. A coating of silver will not protect a material from attack by oxygen. In oxygen-rich environments such as blood, however, silver can soak up the oxygen. This makes silver poisonous to bacteria that need oxygen to survive. So some silver compounds are useful antibacterial drugs.

Where is silver found?

A miner checks the shaft of a drill at a mine for silver, lead, and zinc ores in Idaho.

S ilver is a rare metal and makes up very little of Earth's crust. Pure deposits of silver do exist, but the element is usually found combined with other elements in the form of compounds. Chemical processing is needed to extract pure silver from these compounds and the minerals (rocks) in which they are found. The most important silver mineral is called argentine (silver sulfide, Ag_2S). Silver is also found combined with lead and copper ores and as electrum—a naturally occurring blend of gold and silver.

Silver is one of the oldest known metals. By 2000 B.C.E., mining and smelting of silver-bearing lead ores was common. The Laurium silver-lead deposit in ancient Greece was a major source of silver from

500 B.C.E. to 100 C.E. By the sixteenth century, Spanish conquistadors (explorers) discovered silver mines in Bolivia, Mexico, and Peru. These New World mines were much richer in silver. As a result, South and Central America became one of the largest silver-producing areas in the world. A valuable silver deposit called the Comstock lode is also found in the Sierra Nevada region, making the United States another major silver-producing country.

SILVER FACTS	
Country	Tons of silver produced in the year 2000
Mexico	3,024
Peru	2,688
Australia	2,270
United States	2,171
China	1,653
Canada	1,292
Chile	1,289
Poland	1,258
Bolivia	484

Extracting silver from its ores

Only 25 percent of the silver produced from rocks comes from ores mined solely for the silver they contain. The rest is taken from ores that contain useful amounts of other metals, in particular copper, lead, and zinc. Copper is present as the mineral chalcopyrite ($CuFeS_2$), lead as galena (PbS), and zinc as sphalerite (ZnS). All these deposits contain sulfur and are called sulfides. The ancient Greek deposits at Laurium were mainly used to extract silver associated with the lead ore galena. Lead was also useful to the ancient Greeks, so extracting both metals at the same time made it very profitable.

During the Spanish exploration of the Americas, an open-air method called the patio process was used to extract silver. The patio process involved grinding a silver-bearing ore (containing silver sulfide, Ag_2S) and adding salt (sodium chloride, $NaCl$) and mercury (Hg). Mules were tied to a wooden post on a paved patio and made to walk in a circle through the rock mixture. As the mules trampled on the rocks, they crushed them into fine particles. The warm climate helped a series of chemical reactions to occur. First, the silver sulfide reacted with the sodium chloride to form silver chloride ($AgCl$) and sodium sulfate (Na_2SO_4). Then the silver chloride reacted with the mercury to form mercury chloride ($HgCl$) and pure silver metal. As there was far more mercury than silver, the silver dissolved in the unreacted mercury, forming a liquid amalgam (metal dissolved in mercury). The silver in this amalgam was recovered by distillation. The mercury was collected and used again.

Modern methods of silver extraction are quite different. Because silver is obtained as a by-product of the production of a range of metal ores, a number of chemical

A sixteenth-century silver mine in Germany. At this time, the most important source of silver-bearing ores came from the Spanish exploration of the Americas.

DID YOU KNOW?

RECYCLING SILVER

In 2000, over 18,000 tons (17,640 tonnes) of silver were produced from mining alone. In addition, another 5,600 tons (5,500 tonnes) were produced through recycling silver from scrap. By far the most important source of this recycled silver comes from the photographic industry. Silver can be recycled from spent photographic-processing solutions or from photographic film. So the photographer's shots that do not get developed may end up as a silver bracelet or another item made from silver.

processes can be used to extract the silver. A process called cyanidation is used when the silver is extracted as a by-product of gold production. First, the rock containing the gold- and silver-bearing minerals is crushed, ground, and mixed with a solution of sodium cyanide (NaCN).

Pure silver forms twisted, wirelike formations on a rock. Most silver in nature is found combined with other elements in the form of compounds.

The sodium cyanide reacts with the gold and the silver, forming a complex molecule made up of gold, silver, and sodium atoms. When finely ground zinc powder is added, the silver and gold form an alloy. This is collected and treated to separate the gold and silver.

A sample of the mineral galena, or lead sulfide (PbS), one of the many metal sulfide ores associated with silver ores.

Silver purity

Almost all the silver extracted from ores is refined to make it very pure. The final refining stage uses electricity (a flow of electrons) to purify the silver in a process called electrolysis. First, the impure silver is changed chemically into silver nitrate ($AgNO_3$). Silver nitrate dissolves in water to form silver ions (Ag^+) and nitrate ions (NO^{3-}), which can move freely in the solution. As the electricity passes through the solution, the silver ions move toward the negative electrode. Here, each one gains an electron to become an atom of silver. The atoms stick to the electrode to form a mass of silver that is over 99.9 percent pure.

The refined silver may be kept as a pure metal, but it is often mixed with other metals to improve its hardness or other

A medieval assayer searches for traces of gold in a silver ore. Another worker washes the ore.

characteristics. Silver is very expensive, so the amount of silver mixed with other metals is carefully controlled. In Britain, there are four different levels of purity. Each one is called a fineness level. The lowest level is a fineness of 800, which means that the material contains 800 parts of silver per thousand (80 percent). The highest level is 999 fineness (99.9 percent). In between is sterling silver—the standard grade for decorative silverware—at a fineness of 925.

Hallmarking

Since silver is such a precious metal, it has always been important to know for certain exactly how much silver a piece of the metal contains. This procedure is called

---

DID YOU KNOW?

STERLING SILVER

Sterling silver gave its name to the British system of currency—officially known as pounds sterling. During the reign of Elizabeth I (1558–1603), silver coins were made of sterling silver. No one knows for sure where the word *sterling* originated, but it may have been from the old English word *steorling,* meaning "coin with a star." This was the name of the small star-marked silver coins used during the Norman occupation of England in medieval times.

---

assaying. The system used in England dates back to the fourteenth century. Assays were done by weighing a small sample from the item of silverware, then refining the sample to obtain pure silver. From the weight of the silver obtained, the assayer could work out the purity of the original sample and thus the purity of the item as a whole. Once the purity had been worked out, the assayer stamped the silverware

The four hallmarks shown on the lid of this silver box indicate the purity of silver from which it is made.

with symbols called hallmarks to show the fineness, the manufacturer's initials, and the place of hallmarking. If the tested purity of the item fell between two purity levels, the hallmark showed the lower level. Any item that fell below the minimum purity level was broken up and returned to the silver manufacturer for further refining.

Hallmarks are still used in England and several other European countries. In the United States, there is no national purity testing system. Each manufacturer stamps their own mark to show the silver purity.

Silver alloys

Silver is relatively soft as a pure metal, so it is often mixed with other metals to form alloys. Sterling silver is an alloy of silver and copper. It is strong but retains the glistening white color of pure silver. Many combinations of silver and other metals have been used to make coins. The ancient alloy called electrum was made of a mixture of silver and gold. Because it contained gold, this alloy was even more valuable than pure silver. Most alloys are made with cheaper metals, such as copper or nickel, to imitate the appearance and weight of silver while using less of the precious metal.

Silver alloys may be used in a number of different ways. Often the alloy exhibits remarkably different properties from the metals from which it is made. The melting point of pure silver is 1,763° F (962° C), but silver-based alloys with melting points ranging from 290° F (143° C) to over 1,830° F (1,000° C) have been made. Other silver alloys are produced for specific purposes. For example, an alloy of silver and the precious metal palladium forms a material that allows hydrogen gas to pass through it. Some silver alloys containing copper or nickel and aluminum are used to make electrical parts that work well at extremely high temperatures.

DID YOU KNOW?

SILVER FILLINGS
Many people have a silver alloy in their mouth. Until very recently, dentists used a silvery material called amalgam to fill decayed teeth. Amalgam is an alloy containing up to 70 percent silver, with smaller amounts of copper, tin, zinc, and the liquid metal mercury. The dentist mixed the powdered metals with the liquid mercury. The mixture had the useful property of being soft and malleable when freshly made, but quickly hardened in the tooth to give it a protective covering. There are drawbacks to amalgam fillings. Mercury is poisonous to people, and the amalgam fillings turned black with time. So modern fillings are made of different materials.

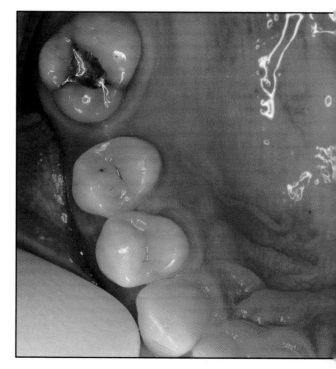

The silver alloy called dental amalgam consists mainly of silver mixed with mercury and smaller quantities of the metals tin, copper, and zinc.

How silver reacts

A silver kettle has tarnished slowly as sulfur compounds in the atmosphere react with the silver surface to form black silver sulfide (Ag_2S).

Silver is fairly unreactive. Unlike most other metals, it does not react with oxygen in the air. Over time, however, silver will lose its shiny white appearance. A brown tarnish of silver sulfide (Ag_2S) forms on the surface of the metal because silver reacts with sulfur compounds in the air. This same reaction causes silver or silver-plated cutlery to tarnish. Raw egg yolk also contains sulfur compounds and can turn a silver spoon almost black. Silver will also react with another gas present in the air—ozone (O_3)—to form silver oxide (Ag_2O).

Silver can form a variety of different compounds with the same element. In the laboratory, silver reacts with oxygen in different ways. Usually it forms oxides with the formulae Ag_2O or AgO, both of which are used to make miniature batteries for cameras and watches. However, another oxide, Ag_2O_3, can also be produced. This oxide is unstable and soon falls apart.

Silver returns to its uncombined metallic state quite easily. As a result, silver compounds are a useful way of testing for substances called "reducing agents"— chemicals whose atoms give up their electrons in chemical reactions. When a reducing agent comes into contact with silver ions, it gives up electrons to the silver ions. Silver atoms form and show up as a silvery lining inside a test tube. This is the

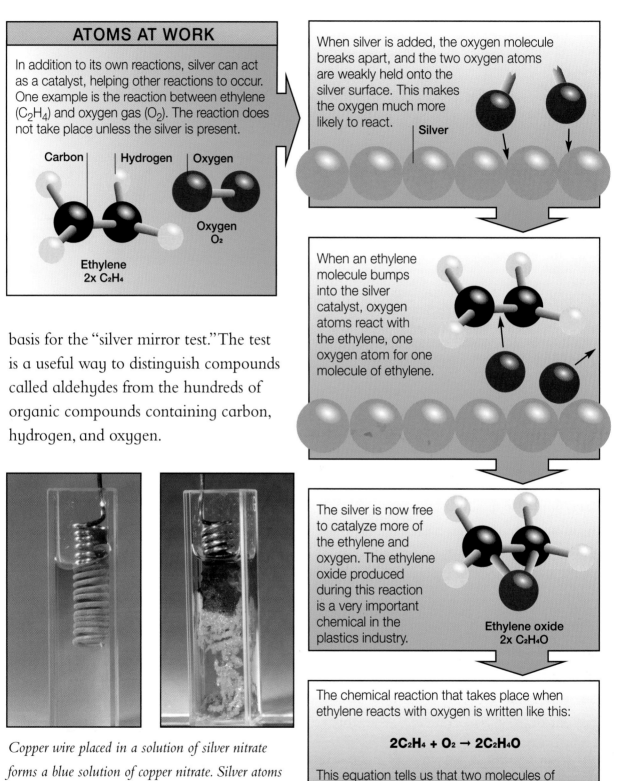

ATOMS AT WORK

In addition to its own reactions, silver can act as a catalyst, helping other reactions to occur. One example is the reaction between ethylene (C_2H_4) and oxygen gas (O_2). The reaction does not take place unless the silver is present.

Carbon | Hydrogen | Oxygen

Oxygen
O_2

Ethylene
2x C_2H_4

When silver is added, the oxygen molecule breaks apart, and the two oxygen atoms are weakly held onto the silver surface. This makes the oxygen much more likely to react.

Silver

When an ethylene molecule bumps into the silver catalyst, oxygen atoms react with the ethylene, one oxygen atom for one molecule of ethylene.

The silver is now free to catalyze more of the ethylene and oxygen. The ethylene oxide produced during this reaction is a very important chemical in the plastics industry.

Ethylene oxide
2x C_2H_4O

The chemical reaction that takes place when ethylene reacts with oxygen is written like this:

$$2C_2H_4 + O_2 \rightarrow 2C_2H_4O$$

This equation tells us that two molecules of ethylene react with one molecule of oxygen to form two molecules of ethylene oxide.

basis for the "silver mirror test." The test is a useful way to distinguish compounds called aldehydes from the hundreds of organic compounds containing carbon, hydrogen, and oxygen.

Copper wire placed in a solution of silver nitrate forms a blue solution of copper nitrate. Silver atoms exchange with copper atoms in the wire, forming a solid silver coating on the wire (right).

ATOMS AT WORK

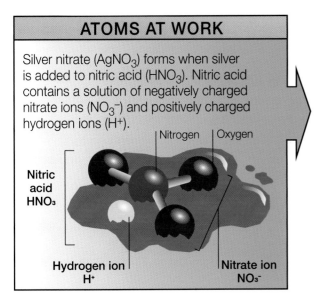

Silver nitrate ($AgNO_3$) forms when silver is added to nitric acid (HNO_3). Nitric acid contains a solution of negatively charged nitrate ions (NO_3^-) and positively charged hydrogen ions (H^+).

Nitrogen | Oxygen

Nitric acid HNO_3

Hydrogen ion H^+

Nitrate ion NO_3^-

Sensitive to light

One popular compound of silver is silver nitrate ($AgNO_3$). Silver nitrate forms when silver metal reacts with nitric acid (HNO_3). This reaction will occur even if the acid is dilute. Silver nitrate must be kept in a dark bottle to keep light out. Light makes the silver nitrate break down into pure metal.

Many other silver compounds are sensitive to light. For example, silver carbonate (Ag_2CO_3) changes color when light shines on it. The compounds that silver forms with the halogen elements—silver chloride ($AgCl$), silver bromide ($AgBr$), and silver iodide (AgI)—are also very sensitive to light. For this reason, silver halides have important uses in the photographic industry. They are used to make photographic developing solutions and photographic film.

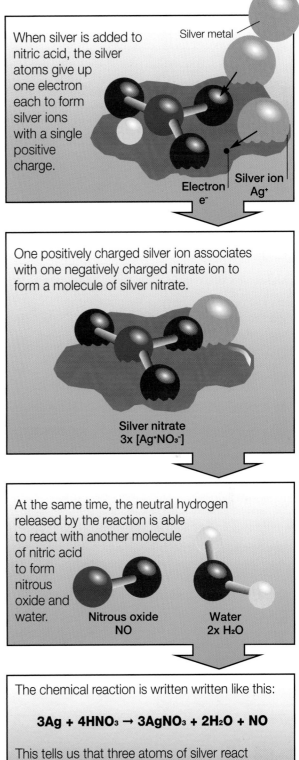

When silver is added to nitric acid, the silver atoms give up one electron each to form silver ions with a single positive charge.

Silver metal

Electron e^-

Silver ion Ag^+

One positively charged silver ion associates with one negatively charged nitrate ion to form a molecule of silver nitrate.

Silver nitrate 3x [$Ag^+NO_3^-$]

At the same time, the neutral hydrogen released by the reaction is able to react with another molecule of nitric acid to form nitrous oxide and water.

Nitrous oxide NO

Water 2x H_2O

The chemical reaction is written written like this:

$$3Ag + 4HNO_3 \rightarrow 3AgNO_3 + 2H_2O + NO$$

This tells us that three atoms of silver react with four molecules of nitric acid to form three molecules of silver nitrate, two molecules of water, and one molecule of nitrous oxide.

Silver and money

Long before true coins were developed, pieces of silver and gold were used as high-value tokens of trade. The ancient Egyptians were the first people to use precious metals in this way around 3000 B.C.E. It took another 2,500 years before the first true coins were issued by a ruler and were stamped to indicate his authority. The first coins were made of electrum—a naturally occurring alloy of silver and gold. By 500 B.C.E., Greece and several other countries by the Mediterranean Sea made and used both silver and gold coins. By 150 B.C.E., the Roman silver *denarius* was the main currency in the Mediterranean area.

From the end of the Roman Empire, right up until the sixteenth century, a shortage of gold in Europe meant that almost all coins were made of silver. The Spanish exploration of the Americas (which began in 1492) meant that more gold and silver became available. The countries of South America, in particular, contained rich supplies of gold and silver. The dollar was introduced at this time—a silver Spanish coin whose name came from the Austrian silver coin known as a "taler."

These ancient, irregularly shaped coins from Anatolia (present-day Turkey) are made of electrum—an alloy of gold and silver.

> ## DID YOU KNOW?
>
> ### SILVER VERSUS GOLD
> The early ancient Egyptians valued silver more than gold. Much more pure gold occurs in nature. Silver is found combined with other elements. The early ancient Egyptians did not know how to extract silver from its ores. Over time, people found more ways to extract silver from its ores, and the value of this metal dropped below that of gold. Today, gold (by weight) is worth about sixteen times more than silver.

These silver coins and bar are marked with a fineness level of 999, which means they are 99.9 percent pure. Each coin weighs one troy ounce, which is the equivalent of just under ²/₂₅ lb (31 g). The bar weighs 100 troy ounces (around 8 lb or 3.1 kg).

The first U. S. silver coin—known as the half-dime—was minted in 1792. In the United States and Europe throughout the twentieth century, the proportion of silver in the silver coins was reduced in stages as the price of silver increased. Silver was eliminated completely from U. S. currency in 1965. Only one country—Mexico—still uses silver in the coins in general circulation. In many countries, however, silver is just used to make commemorative coins.

The mirror of Princess Sathathoryunet from the twelfth dynasty of the ancient Egyptian New Kingdom dates back over 3,500 years. The surface of the mirror is made of a reflective layer of pure silver.

Most of the silverware after the time of the Roman Empire, right up until medieval times, was made for religious purposes. Around 1330, silver compounds were used to color the stained glass of many Gothic cathedrals. Silver sulfide was applied to clear glass. Heating the stained glass would yield a range of colors, from canary yellow to rich brown. Around the same time, the craft guilds of silversmiths

Silver and ornaments

The beauty, value, and versatility of silver makes it an ideal material for use in decorative items. In Roman times, silverware was extremely fashionable. One author recorded seeing several dozen silver plates, each of which weighed over 110 lb (50 kg). Roman silverware was highly decorated, often with scenes of heroism.

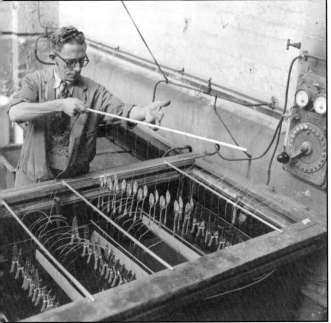

A factory worker in Sheffield, England, removes a batch of silver-plated spoons from an electrolytic cell.

and goldsmiths became a powerful force in many countries in Europe. The strict controls on the quality of silver that were introduced then remain today.

Silver plating

In 1742, an Englishman named Thomas Bolsover accidentally overheated a knife handle made of silver and copper and noticed that the silver formed a layer over the copper. Bolsover realized that he could make silverware with a shiny silver finish at a lower cost than items made of pure silver. He developed a technique to mass-produce the silver-plated copper. Bolsover's technique was called Sheffield Plate after the English industrial town of Sheffield.

ATOMS AT WORK

Silver plating is carried out using a solution of silver cyanide. In the solution, the silver cyanide separates into silver ions (Ag^+) and cyanide ions (CN^-).

Cyanide ion (CN^-)
Silver ion (Ag^+)

The item is placed into the solution and connected to a battery. The item acts as the negative electrode. A piece of silver is fixed to the battery to form the positive electrode.

Metal item
Battery
Piece of silver

As electrons flow along the wire, silver ions move toward the negative electrode (the object to be plated), picking up electrons and forming silver atoms at the object's surface.

$\bar{e}$
$\bar{e}$
Silver plate

The chemical reaction can be written like this:

$$Ag^+ + \bar{e} \rightarrow Ag$$

This equation tells us that one silver ion picks up one electron to form one silver atom.

A silverworker engraves a design onto a silver bowl. Silver is a fairly malleable metal, which means that it is relatively easy to mark with intricate designs.

A few decades later, electroplating was invented. The spread of this technology was so rapid that it replaced the Sheffield Plate in a matter of years.

Today, silver remains a very popular metal for decorative items such as jewelry. In 2000, over 9,580 tons (8,700 tonnes) of silver were used to make items such as rings, bracelets, and necklaces. However, less silver is used to make tableware and cutlery. Silver-plated cutlery is much less expensive than solid silver, but it is still too expensive for many people to buy. The biggest problem is the tarnish that occurs when silver comes into contact with foods containing sulfur compounds. Most people prefer to use stainless steel cutlery instead. Small decorative objects, such as photo frames and candlesticks, however, continue to be popular gifts and treasured ornaments in many homes.

DID YOU KNOW?

SILVER WORKING

Many different techniques have been used to make silver jewelry over the centuries and many are still in use today. Silver wire is the starting point for making chains of all degrees of weight or delicacy. In filigree work, designs are created from a very fine silver wire and tiny silver beads are often added. For other items, silver is cast from molten metal or shaped from flat sheets. Regardless of the method used, the silver first needs to be softened by a process called annealing. In this process, the silver is heated and then slowly cooled. This allows the silver atoms to arrange themselves into tiny crystals that can slide over each other very easily. After annealing, the silver can be hammered or worked into the required shape. The hammering process also hardens the silver so that it retains its shape and durability afterward.

Silver in photography

It had been known for centuries that silver compounds darken when exposed to light. But the first person to use this property to produce a photographic image was German physicist Johann Heinrich Schulze. In 1727, Schulze made a paste of silver nitrate and chalk, placed the mixture in a glass bottle, and wrapped the bottle in a piece of paper in which he had cut out letter shapes. After placing the bottle in sunlight Schultz removed the paper, revealing dark letter shapes where the mixture had been exposed to light.

Unfortunately, Schulze's image was not permanent. Continued exposure to light further darkened the mixture in the bottle. So the search began for a way to capture a permanent image. The idea of capturing a real scene, rather than just a stencil pattern, was also part of the challenge.

In 1839, French painter and physicist Louis-Jacques-Mandé Daguerre (1787–1851) invented the first practical photographic process. Daguerre used a device called a camera obscura to capture an image on a polished copper plate coated

William Henry Fox Talbot (far right) shown at his photographic studio in Reading, England.

DID YOU KNOW?

X RAYS

Silver compounds are also used to produce the X-ray photographs taken in hospitals. X rays and visible light are both forms of electromagnetic radiation. Unlike visible light, however, X rays are invisible and have more energy. Large doses of X-ray radiation can be dangerous to the body. But X rays taken at a hospital are usually harmless. When you have an X ray, the X rays pass though your flesh but not through your bones. When the X-ray picture is developed, what you see is a negative picture. The dark areas, containing the developed silver compound, correspond to where the X rays have hit the film. The light areas on the image correspond to the areas where the X rays were stopped by bone.

Photographs are developed in a darkroom until the image is fixed onto photographic paper.

with silver iodide. Once the picture had been taken, Daguerre immersed the copper plate in mercury vapor. The mercury clung to the parts of the plate exposed to light, revealing the image. The resulting images, called daguerrotypes, made very attractive pictures but were costly. Their use was also limited by the fact that each daguerrotype was unique—copies could not be made of the same daguerrotype.

British chemist William Henry Fox Talbot (1800–1877) solved the problem in 1841. Talbot used paper soaked in light-sensitive silver iodide suspension to form the photographic image. The exposed paper was developed using a chemical called sodium thiosulfite or "hypo" ($Na_2S_2O_3$). The hypo acts by dissolving any silver iodide left unchanged by the light. Copies could be printed from the "negative" images on the paper.

Further refinements to the photographic process were made in the nineteenth century. For example, the paper used by Talbot was replaced with glass to produce a more detailed image. Photographers also looked to decrease the exposure time by finding chemical ways to "sensitize" the silver compound used. Silver bromide was found to be much more sensitive to light. The development of photographic film followed the invention of a plastic called celluloid in 1873. In 1888, the American founder of the Eastman Kodak company George Eastman (1854–1932) finally brought photography to the masses when he launched the Kodak camera in 1888.

Around 7,700 tons (7,000 tonnes) of silver is consumed by the photographic industry worldwide every year. All the silver used in this industry is up to 99.99 percent pure. However, digital-imaging technology has become more popular. Digital images are recorded electronically rather than on film. As a result, this may soon lead to a reduction in the amount of silver used by the photographic industry.

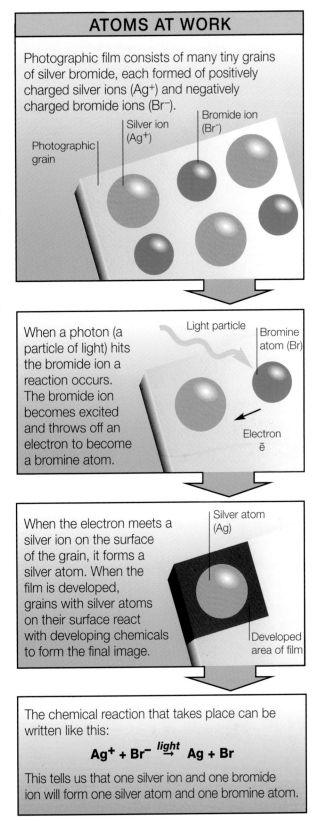

ATOMS AT WORK

Photographic film consists of many tiny grains of silver bromide, each formed of positively charged silver ions (Ag^+) and negatively charged bromide ions (Br^-).

Photographic grain
Silver ion (Ag^+)
Bromide ion (Br^-)

When a photon (a particle of light) hits the bromide ion a reaction occurs. The bromide ion becomes excited and throws off an electron to become a bromine atom.

Light particle
Bromine atom (Br)
Electron ē

When the electron meets a silver ion on the surface of the grain, it forms a silver atom. When the film is developed, grains with silver atoms on their surface react with developing chemicals to form the final image.

Silver atom (Ag)
Developed area of film

The chemical reaction that takes place can be written like this:

$$Ag^+ + Br^- \overset{light}{\rightarrow} Ag + Br$$

This tells us that one silver ion and one bromide ion will form one silver atom and one bromine atom.

Silver in industry

Silver is used in modern electronics as a soldering material. A heating element melts the silver, which hardens to join electrical components.

Silver is a very expensive metal, but it still has many uses in industry and in products for the home. One of the main uses of silver comes from the fact that it conducts electricity better than any other element. As a result, it is used in many electrical and electronic devices. In many computer keyboards, for example, silver is the substance that registers a keystroke in the form of an electrical pulse. These so-called membrane switches consist of two pieces of tough fabric coated with silver. When you depress a key, the sheets touch, contact is made, and an electrical current flows. Switches containing silver contacts are also used in other electrical equipment in the home. Some examples are wall switches, washing machines, and microwaves. In addition, silver is very hard-wearing and is very resistant to corrosion.

Silver is also used to make batteries that store lots of energy in a small space. The tiny circular batteries used in watches and hearing aids are silver oxide–zinc cells, which contain around 35 percent silver. The ability of silver batteries to store lots of energy in a small space has led to their use onboard spacecraft—to power doors and other devices. The batteries are even used inside space suits and the life-sustaining gear used in spacewalking.

Many of silver's uses in industry also depend on its decorative qualities. For example, many mirrors are manufactured using a very thin layer of silver as the reflective material. The silver is applied to a flat surface of glass by a chemical reaction between silver nitrate and a chemical reducing agent. The reducing agent donates electrons to the silver ion in the silver compound. The silver ion then changes into metallic silver, which sticks to the glass. A backing is then added to prevent the silver from tarnishing or wearing away and to stop light from being transmitted through the thin layer.

DID YOU KNOW?

HEAT PROTECTION

Silver is an excellent reflector of light, and it is also extremely resistant to corrosion. For these reasons, silver was used to coat the quartz tiles on the Magellan spacecraft. The silver coating protected the spacecraft from the Sun's rays as the spacecraft orbited the surface of Venus. Because of the proximity of Venus to the Sun, during the orbit the Magellan spacecraft faced over two times the levels of solar radiation than a near-Earth orbit. As a result, over 24,000 silver-coated tiles were used to keep the spacecraft's delicate electronics from overheating. Following the same principle, silver-coated glass—which reflects a large proportion of sunlight—is now available for use in buildings and cars in hot climates. This reduces the need for expensive air-conditioning systems.

Some other uses of silver make our lives much safer. For example, silver-coated bearings are used in aircraft engines. If the lubrication system fails, silver is "slippery" enough to allow the aircraft engine to be shut down safely. And in automobiles the heaters that stop ice from forming on the rear windshield consist of small grains of silver oxide bonded to the glass by heat.

The solar array wing panel of the International Space Station. Silver is used to make the electrical connection between solar cells and the wires that carry the light-generated electricity to where it is needed.

Silver in health

Silver has been used for thousands of years to prevent infection. It is well documented that silver was used in ancient Greece and Rome as a disinfectant for water and other liquid storage. Silver took an official place in medicine in 1884, when German physician F. Crede used a solution of silver nitrate as an eyedrop for newborns. Crede virtually eliminated infant blindness. As a result, the treatment continued right up until antibiotics were developed in the 1940s.

Silver and its compounds are still valued for their powerful germ-killing effects. In addition to its recognized antibacterial properties, a compound called silver sulfadiazine helps to regenerate damaged tissue in major burns, where the wounds are no longer protected by the skin. Some physicians also think that silver might play a role in the prevention of cancer. Silver metal was also once used in the body as wire for keeping broken bones in place and as plates for bone replacement.

How silver works

Silver kills disease-causing bacteria by inactivating the enzymes involved in respiration. Just one part per 100 million

Silver compounds have been used as an alternative to antibiotics in chicken farming. The chemicals help to keep the birds free from bacterial infection and therefore safe to eat. This is one way to prevent the overuse of antibiotics.

DID YOU KNOW?

PURE WATER

The power of silver to purify water has been known since the time of the Phoenicians—a seafaring nation that thrived during the time of the ancient Greeks. To preserve the drinks, the Phoenicians carried water and wine in silver-lined vessels on long voyages. Similarly, the first settlers of the United States put silver coins in water barrels to keep the water fresh. More recently, the National Space and Aeronautics Administration (NASA) uses silver to keep water pure on the space shuttle. The water systems of large buildings, such as hospitals, use silver to prevent a bacterial infection called Legionnaire's disease. Silver is also used in household water filters to keep the water free from bacteria.

of elemental silver is effective. The unreactive nature of silver means that it should not harm the body. Unlike many modern antibiotics, there is no known bacterial resistance to silver.

Silver does have some drawbacks. Some silver compounds, especially silver nitrate, stain the skin. Others can be harmful if they enter the body in anything above small amounts. For the most part, however, silver is safe in small doses, giving it a value way beyond its high price.

Silver compounds are now being used as an alternative to chlorine to keep pools free from harmful bacteria. The same silver compounds are also added to drinking water supply systems.

Periodic table

Everything in the universe consists of combinations of substances called elements. Elements are made of tiny atoms, which are too small to see. Atoms are the building blocks of matter.

The character of an atom depends on how many even tinier particles (called protons) there are in its center, or nucleus. An element's atomic number is the same as the number of its protons.

Scientists have found around 110 different elements. About 90 elements occur naturally on Earth. The rest have been made in experiments.

All these elements are set out on a chart called the periodic table. This lists all the elements in order according to their atomic number.

The elements at the left of the table are metals. Those at the right are nonmetals. Between the metals and the nonmetals are the metalloids, which sometimes act like metals and sometimes like nonmetals.

- On the left of the table are the alkali metals. These elements have just one electron in their outer shells.
- On the right of the periodic table are the noble gases. These elements have full outer shells.
- Elements in the same group have the same number of electrons in their outer shells.

- Elements get more reactive as you go down a group.
- The number of electrons orbiting the nucleus increases down each group.
- The transition metals are in the middle of the table, between Groups II and III.

Group I

Group II

Transition metals

1 **H** Hydrogen 1								
3 **Li** Lithium 7	4 **Be** Beryllium 9							
11 **Na** Sodium 23	12 **Mg** Magnesium 24							
19 **K** Potassium 39	20 **Ca** Calcium 40	21 **Sc** Scandium 45	22 **Ti** Titanium 48	23 **V** Vanadium 51	24 **Cr** Chromium 52	25 **Mn** Manganese 55	26 **Fe** Iron 56	27 **Co** Cobalt 59
37 **Rb** Rubidium 85	38 **Sr** Strontium 88	39 **Y** Yttrium 89	40 **Zr** Zirconium 91	41 **Nb** Niobium 93	42 **Mo** Molybdenum 96	43 **Tc** Technetium (98)	44 **Ru** Ruthenium 101	45 **Rh** Rhodium 103
55 **Cs** Cesium 133	56 **Ba** Barium 137	71 **Lu** Lutetium 175	72 **Hf** Hafnium 179	73 **Ta** Tantalum 181	74 **W** Tungsten 184	75 **Re** Rhenium 186	76 **Os** Osmium 190	77 **Ir** Iridium 192
87 **Fr** Francium 223	88 **Ra** Radium 226	103 **Lr** Lawrencium (260)	104 **Unq** Unnilquadium (261)	105 **Unp** Unnilpentium (262)	106 **Unh** Unnilhexium (263)	107 **Uns** Unnilseptium (?)	108 **Uno** Unniloctium (?)	109 **Une** Unnilennium (?)

Lanthanide elements

Actinide elements

57 **La** Lanthanum 139	58 **Ce** Cerium 140	59 **Pr** Praseodymium 141	60 **Nd** Neodymium 144	61 **Pm** Promethium (145)
89 **Ac** Actinium 227	90 **Th** Thorium 232	91 **Pa** Protactinium 231	92 **U** Uranium 238	93 **Np** Neptunium (237)

The horizontal rows are called periods. As you go across a period, the atomic number increases by one from each element to the next. The vertical columns are called groups. Elements get heavier as you go down a group. All the elements in a group have the same number of electrons in their outer shells. This means they react in similar ways.

The transition metals fall between Groups II and III. Their electron shells fill up in an unusual way. The lanthanide elements and the actinide elements are set apart from the main table to make it easier to read. All the lanthanide elements and the actinide elements are quite rare.

Silver in the table

Silver's atomic number is 47, so it has 47 protons in its nucleus. This element is positioned in the middle of the periodic table in a group known as the transition elements. Like many metals, silver is shiny and a good conductor of electricity and heat. Unlike most metals, it is unreactive, which is why it is so highly prized.

■ Metals
■ Metalloids (semimetals)
■ Nonmetals

| 47 |
| Ag |
| Silver |
| 108 |

Atomic (proton) number
Symbol
Name
Atomic mass

Group VIII

			Group III	**Group IV**	**Group V**	**Group VI**	**Group VII**	2 He Helium 4
			5 B Boron 11	6 C Carbon 12	7 N Nitrogen 14	8 O Oxygen 16	9 F Fluorine 19	10 Ne Neon 20
			13 Al Aluminum 27	14 Si Silicon 28	15 P Phosphorus 31	16 S Sulfur 32	17 Cl Chlorine 35	18 Ar Argon 40
28 Ni Nickel 59	29 Cu Copper 64	30 Zn Zinc 65	31 Ga Gallium 70	32 Ge Germanium 73	33 As Arsenic 75	34 Se Selenium 79	35 Br Bromine 80	36 Kr Krypton 84
46 Pd Palladium 106	47 Ag Silver 108	48 Cd Cadmium 112	49 In Indium 115	50 Sn Tin 119	51 Sb Antimony 122	52 Te Tellurium 128	53 I Iodine 127	54 Xe Xenon 131
78 Pt Platinum 195	79 Au Gold 197	80 Hg Mercury 201	81 Tl Thallium 204	82 Pb Lead 207	83 Bi Bismuth 209	84 Po Polonium (209)	85 At Astatine (210)	86 Rn Radon (222)

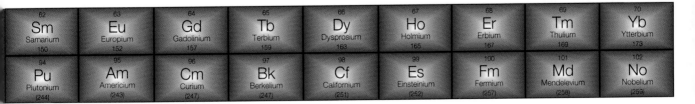

62 Sm Samarium 150	63 Eu Europium 152	64 Gd Gadolinium 157	65 Tb Terbium 159	66 Dy Dysprosium 163	67 Ho Holmium 165	68 Er Erbium 167	69 Tm Thulium 169	70 Yb Ytterbium 173
94 Pu Plutonium (244)	95 Am Americium (243)	96 Cm Curium (247)	97 Bk Berkelium (247)	98 Cf Californium (251)	99 Es Einsteinium (252)	100 Fm Fermium (257)	101 Md Mendelevium (258)	102 No Nobelium (259)

Chemical reactions

Chemical reactions are going on all the time—candles burn, nails rust, food is digested. Some reactions involve just two substances; others many more. But whenever a reaction takes place, at least one substance is changed.

In a chemical reaction, the atoms stay the same. But they join up in different combinations to form new molecules.

Writing an equation

Chemical reactions can be described by writing down the atoms and molecules before the reaction and the atoms and molecules after. Since the atoms stay the

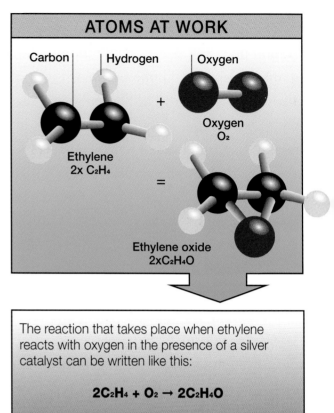

ATOMS AT WORK

Carbon | Hydrogen | Oxygen

Oxygen
O_2

Ethylene
$2x\ C_2H_4$

Ethylene oxide
$2xC_2H_4O$

The reaction that takes place when ethylene reacts with oxygen in the presence of a silver catalyst can be written like this:

$$2C_2H_4 + O_2 \rightarrow 2C_2H_4O$$

same, the number of atoms before will be the same as the number of atoms after. Chemists write down an equation to show what happens in the chemical reaction.

Making it balance

When the numbers of each atom on both sides of the equation are equal, the equation is balanced. If the numbers are not equal, something is wrong. So the chemist adjusts the number of atoms involved until the equation does balance.

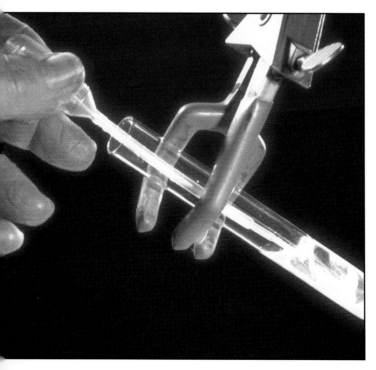

A cloudy white precipitate (a solid) of silver chloride (AgCl) is formed during the reaction of sodium chloride (NaCl) and silver nitrate ($AgNO_3$).

Glossary

alloy: A mixture of a metal with one or more other elements.

antibiotic: A drug that kills or prevents the growth of bacteria.

atom: The smallest part of an element that has all the properties of that element.

atomic mass: The number of protons and neutrons in an atom.

atomic number: The number of protons in an atom.

bond: The attraction between two atoms, or ions, that holds them together.

catalyst: Something that makes a chemical reaction occur more quickly.

compound: A substance made of two or more elements bonded together.

corrosion: The eating away of a material by reaction with other chemicals.

electrode: A material that is used to conduct an electrical current to or from an object.

electrolysis: The use of electricity to change a substance chemically.

electron: A tiny particle with a negative charge. Electrons orbit the nucleus of an atom in layers called electron shells.

electroplating: The process of using electricity to put a thin layer of one metal on top of another.

element: A substance that is made from only one type of atom.

fineness: A measure of the purity of silver. It tells you how many parts per thousand of a silver object are pure silver.

hallmark: A marking stamped on a silver (or gold) object, verifying it as genuine.

ion: An atom that has lost or gained electrons. Ions have either a positive or negative electrical charge.

isotopes: Atoms of an element with the same number of protons and electrons but different numbers of neutrons.

molecule: A particle that contains atoms held together by chemical bonds.

neutron: A tiny particle with no electrical charge. Neutrons are found in the nucleus of every atom except hydrogen.

nucleus: The dense structure at the center of an atom.

ore: A compound that contains a useful element, usually a metal, mixed together with other elements.

periodic table: A chart of all the chemical elements laid out in order of their atomic number.

proton: A tiny particle with a positive charge found in the nucleus of all atoms.

refining: An industrial process that frees elements, such as metals, from impurities or unwanted material.

troy ounce: A traditional measure of the weight of silver. One troy ounce equals 1.097 ordinary ounces or 31.10 grams.

X ray: A form of radiation similar to light but invisible to the naked eye.

Index